MW00775037

THE THRIVAL MAN
30-DAY DEVOTIONAL

The Thrival Man 30-Day Devotional

Eric Eaton

ISBN: 978-1-64184-955-5 (Paperback)
ISBN: 978-1-64184-956-2 (Ebook)
Eaton Creative Arts, LLC. Crested Butte, CO

The Internet addresses in this book are accurate at the time of
publication. They are provided as a resource. Eric Eaton and the
publisher do not endorse them or vouch for their content or
permanence.

To protect the privacy of those who have shared their stories
with the author, some details and names have been changed.

For every man who longs for a more abundant life!

CONTENTS

"Most men live lives of quiet desperation and go to the grave with the song still in them."

Henry David Thoreau

INTRODUCTION

I have spent most of my adult life counseling and coaching men. Over this 25-year span, I have found that there are two questions men deal with on one level or another: "What does it mean to be a man?" and "How do I spend time with God?" The Thrival Man Devotional is a response to both of these questions.

First off, this devotional provides a Biblical perspective to what it means to be a godly man in today's modern world. A Thrival Man is someone who chooses not to just survive life based upon the world's standards, simply hoping for something better to come along. A Thrival Man is a man who chooses to live a thriving life in spite of the circumstances around him—what Jesus, in John 10:10, refers to as the "abundant" life He came to give us.

In regard to the second question, when I ask men why they don't spend time with God, the most common responses are: "I don't know what to do" or "I don't have time." The Thrival Man Devotional also addresses these concerns. It provides content you can walk through on a daily basis. And you only need to carve out 15 minutes of your day to complete the devotional.

The bottom line is, this world is in desperate need of more godly men who are constantly and consistently pursuing Christ—men who refuse to live by the world's standards and definitions of what it means to be a man.

Over the many years we have run the Knights of Heroes camp for children of fallen soldiers, I have seen firsthand the challenges of not having a father and husband around directly affects the family. The lack of confidence in the children is staggering. Plus, the desire to have some man speak into their lives is overwhelming.

This same scenario is being repeated all across the world in various forms. Which is why the world needs you to be a Thrival Man. Use the next 30 days to commit to a true transformation in your life: to throw off your old way of living for Self and choose to live a life fully built on the foundation of Jesus Christ. There is nothing more important you can do over the next 30 days.

For the sake of your life, your family, and this world we live in, let's raise up a new generation of men who choose to live a thriving life. A life of abundance in a world of chaos.

Note: I have put the Bible verses in each day without the passages to encourage you to go to the Word. Open your Bibles each morning, read the passage, and study the contents deeply. Use these 30 days to get deeper in the Word as you pursue transformation in Christ.

DAY 1

THE DEFINITION OF A GODLY MAN

1 Corinthians 16:13-14

Our modern society has muddied the waters when it comes to the definition of a man. From toxic masculinity, radical feminism, Hollywood actions films, and the feminization of man—all of which are very poor characterizations of a true man of God. The problem is, we need more true men in our families, churches, and communities, but most men simply have no clue what being a godly man means.

How did you learn to be a man? Was it from your father, on television, within the community, or from watching other men? Who influenced you to become the man you are today? To become the man we need to be, we must first deconstruct much of what we have learned about being the man we are now.

The Biblical definition of a man and the example given to us of what it means to be a man through Jesus Christ are radically different than the world's definition.

Throughout this devotional, take the time to journal, think, process, and most importantly, implement the Biblical perspectives on being a man. The more you put into transforming into the man God created you to be, the more you will truly become the man God sees in you.

Journal: Where did you learn the traits of being the man you are today? What are the positive and negative aspects of those traits? Write out your definition of being a man. What are the defining traits?

_____

_____

_____

_____

_____

_____

_____

_____

_____

_____

_____

_____

_____

_____

_____

_____

_____

_____

_____

_____

Prayer: Pray today that your heart, soul, mind, and body would be tuned to transform into the man God created you to be. Ask for a humble heart to become a godly man.

DAY 2

WHY WE NEED GODLY MEN

Ephesians 6:10

The role of men has been minimized lately to the point of stating we're no longer relevant. This, of course, is a lie perpetrated by the enemy to take the men out of the game. For if the man is not around, the repercussions can reverberate for generations.

Every year, at the Knights of Heroes camp, I've witnessed firsthand what the impact of not having a father figure around has on young boys and girls. They're desperate for the attention of a man because it's built into their DNA. Without a solid man investing in their lives, they'll search for it elsewhere. Usually in places that are unhealthy and at times destructive.

More godly men in our families will begin to create a stronger presence in our churches. This will have the effect of creating stronger communities of men coming together for a greater purpose and passion. Can you imagine how one community could be completely transformed if just a few men decided to live all out for Jesus Christ?

Don't discount your role as a man and your purpose in our society. Stop believing the lies perpetrated by the enemy about your importance. Rise up to take claim of a role uniquely designed just for you.

Journal: How have you seen godly men make an impact in your own life or the lives of others? How did they make this impact? How could your community be specifically transformed by the investment of more godly men?

_____

_____

_____

_____

_____

_____

_____

_____

_____

_____

_____

_____

_____

_____

_____

_____

_____

Prayer: Pray today for God to begin to stir the hearts of men around you. Either in your neighborhood, work, church, or community. Pray for a revival of men to stand up and claim their place as leaders in the Kingdom of Heaven here on earth.

DAY 3

YOUR RESPONSIBILITY AS A MAN

Ephesians 6:11; 1 Corinthians 16:13

While it may not be easy to see the impact of a man in the lives of those around him, it's easy to see what happens when he is not there.

- Children in father-absent homes are almost four times more likely to be poor. Fatherless children are at a dramatically greater risk of drug and alcohol abuse.
- Children of single-parent homes are more than twice as likely to commit suicide.
- Father involvement in schools is associated with the higher likelihood of getting mostly A's.
- Adolescents living in intact families are less likely to engage in delinquency than their peers living in non-intact families.

As men we can make excuses to go golf, fishing, motorcycle riding, or other activities. But the best place we can spend our time is in our homes with our families. And if you don't have a family, invest in the lives of those kids who don't have a father around.

The more serious we get about our responsibility as men, the better chance we have at not only transforming our own lives but the lives of those around us. This is our responsibility alone to accept and adamantly execute.

Journal: How do you view your responsibility as a man? Is it more self-serving or outward-serving? What are some ways you can take your responsibility as a man more seriously, and what do those activities look like?

_____

_____

_____

_____

_____

_____

_____

_____

_____

_____

_____

_____

_____

_____

_____

_____

_____

_____

Prayer: Let your prayer today be around clarity that you may see your responsibility as a man more clearly. Let God open your eyes and heart to which activities are self-serving and which can be more outward-serving.

DAY 4

THE LEGACY OF A MAN

Proverbs 22:8; Galatians 6:7-10

One reason I write is to leave a legacy for my children. Long after I'm gone I know there will be books, devotionals, and content that my great-great grandchildren can read to know and understand my heart.

The importance of being a Thrival Man after God's own heart is also displayed in the legacy he leaves. A man who is abusive will leave a legacy of abuse. A man who is dishonest will leave a legacy lacking in integrity. A man who is lacking in character will leave a legacy fraught with poor decisions.

But in turn, a man who truly lives with a heart after Christ will leave a lasting legacy. A legacy built upon character, integrity, substance, and truth. This is a legacy which is lacking in our modern society but is not completely lost. We still have the ability to forge this legacy within ourselves and with the men around us.

By choosing to live as a godly man, you are choosing to leave this type of legacy. Begin to think about what this legacy looks like in those who have come before you. And the type of legacy you want to leave not only with your family, but with your church and community.

Journal: Begin by writing out the type of legacy you want to leave behind. What are some specific traits of this legacy? What are the benefits of leaving this legacy behind? Now write out what your current legacy looks like in order to know what you need to do to fill in the gap.

_____

_____

_____

_____

_____

_____

_____

_____

_____

_____

_____

_____

_____

_____

_____

_____

Prayer: Pray today for the strength to stand tall for your legacy. Your legacy will most likely go against everything the world believes in and recognizes. Have the strength to let your legacy in Christ stand no matter what direction the world is moving.

DAY 5

A DAILY CALL

Luke 9:23; 1 Thessalonians 5:17

Have you ever started a workout routine or diet and it was great for a day? But then by day 2 or 3, you have already given up or forgotten about your routine. This is a very common problem with New Year's resolutions. We have the best of intentions but lack determination in the execution of our goals. There is really no one to blame. You get distracted, run out of time, or possibly didn't plan well enough. No matter the cause, the end result of living our old life is always the outcome.

When it comes to our time with God, for the purpose of becoming a better man, we have to look at this differently. This is not a one-time proclamation to transform your life. It is a daily commitment to follow Christ no matter the cost. No matter the circumstances, challenges, or current struggles of life. You get up every day regardless of your circumstances to come before Christ to worship, praise, and learn from the Master.

Much like a workout routine or diet, what you do is less important than creating the environment to make it happen—and actually committing to the daily routine. When it comes to spending time with God, have the same mentality. Create the space, find something to do, and execute the practice daily.

Journal: Do you spend a specific time with God now? Write out when is the best time for you to spend time with God. Write out several topics, books, devotionals, or practices you can commit to during this time. Then begin to create the daily habit of coming before God.

_____

_____

_____

_____

_____

_____

_____

_____

_____

_____

_____

_____

_____

_____

_____

_____

_____

_____

Prayer: Pray today for the perseverance to have a daily practice of coming before God. This will not be an easy task, which is why relying on some supernatural strength in the process is a good idea.

DAY 6

LIKE JESUS

1 Cor. 6:13-14; Hebrews 10:9; 12:3; Matt. 4:1-11

According to these verses, a true man is vigilant against danger, faithful to the truth, brave in the face of opposition, persistent through trials, and, above all, loving. In the attempt to find some characteristics of what it is like to be a "man," the Bible provides the best descriptions.

But the bottom line is, these are not easy traits. If they were, as men, we would all be seeking out these practices. Instead, it is easier to be the jerk, to be selfish in your actions, and only look out for number one. These take absolutely no effort on your part. This is the man we become when we have no meaningful intention or purpose in our lives whatsoever. Essentially the lowest common denominator of being a man.

But we get a very different image in Christ. A man who lived with absolute intention. Who shunned sin, lived for others, cared little about his own self, and ignored what others thought about him—even showing compassion to his accusers while hanging from the cross.

Every day we should be taking a step toward the cross to become more Christ-like.

Journal: What traits of Jesus do you find easy to emulate? Which ones are difficult? What are the steps you need to take today in order to steer your life toward Christ instead of the world?

_____

_____

_____

_____

_____

_____

_____

_____

_____

_____

_____

_____

_____

_____

_____

_____

_____

_____

_____

Prayer: Pray for clarity today to see yourself as the person God created. Not the one the world is telling you to be. Take some quiet time to reflect on the godly man you were created to be.

DAY 7

BE ON GUARD

1 Cor. 16:13; 2 Timothy 3:16-17; Psalms 1

The crux of what Paul is trying to state here is that we need to guard the spiritual part of our lives. We don't need to treat it like some symptom of a cold; we need to attack it like a cancer. We have to understand the importance of our spiritual well-being to ruthlessly guard that part of our lives.

A father and his son were working on a double-sided puzzle. On one side was a map of the world. On the other was a picture of a man. The young boy had put the puzzle together many times before. As his father struggled to find the right place for all the pieces to complete the picture of the world, his son told him to turn all the pieces over, because he had found it was much easier to put the puzzle together by concentrating on the picture of the man. Finishing the puzzle quickly, the boy told his father, "See? When you get the man right, the world is right."

We spend a tremendous amount of time focusing in on the wrong thing. Instead of guarding our hearts against these dangers and focusing in on what matters most, we let the things of this world consume us and distract us from focusing in on the most important thing: living like Christ. How do you need to get the "man" right before concentrating on the rest of the world?

Journal: What do you need to be on guard about when it comes to your spiritual life? Is it your heart, alcohol, porn, a wandering eye, envy of what your neighbor possesses? Do you need to be praying more, studying the Bible, or finding a strong community of men?

_____

_____

_____

_____

_____

_____

_____

_____

_____

_____

_____

_____

_____

_____

_____

_____

_____

_____

Prayer: Pray today that your heart would be guarded—and I mean _fiercely_ guarded—against the attacks of this world. Pray specifically over those areas of your life that are taking you down the wrong path.

DAY 8

WORK ENTHUSIASTICALLY

1 Corinthians 16:13; 15:58; Joshua 24:14-15

Have you ever seen someone work enthusiastically? We had some road construction near our house recently, which is always a frustration. The waiting and inconvenience just to get to your destination is never fun. Except for one man who chose to do his job differently. He was the worker with the sign who got to tell you when to stop and when you could go. But instead of just standing there, this man danced. Danced like no one was watching and waved at everyone who drove past. By his conscious choice to "work enthusiastically," he dramatically changed the negative aspects of the construction while putting a smile on faces.

How enthusiastically could you do the work of Christ if you simply didn't care about what the world thought? If you didn't care about the pursuits of this world and were not distracted by what this world expects of you? It is easy to get caught up in these pursuits because the world sends out a constant consistent message.

When you work for Self or for selfish gains, you'll never have enough or be satisfied. How can you overcome this message, and how is the world being a distraction to you from becoming a man who is enthusiastically working for God?

Journal: What does it look like for you to work enthusiastically, not for yourself but for the kingdom of God?
What are some specific traits you gain by intentionally
choosing to work for a greater cause? Reflect on this and
ensure you are honest with yourself. Your work at your
job may be the only place others will ever see Christ.

_____

_____

_____

_____

_____

_____

_____

_____

_____

_____

_____

_____

_____

_____

_____

_____

_____

_____

_____

Prayer: Pray today for a heart to work enthusiastically.
To shed the labels of what others might think and to live
whole-heartedly for Christ.

DAY 9

STAND FIRM IN THE FAITH

1 Corinthians 16:13; 15:58; Proverbs 25:26

Paul is telling the Corinthians to literally *stand fast, persevere, do not deviate* in their faith and trust. The meaning is deeper than our usual understanding of believing and trusting. In the context of the rest of his letter, Paul is telling the Christians in Corinth to stand firm in the truth that has been revealed to them, stand firm in all that Christ is and all He represents, *the faith which was once and for all delivered* (Jude 3) to the church.

We live in a society that is always chasing the proverbial shiny object. Once our attention spans run short on the current trend, we immediately start looking for the next object to chase. In a constantly changing world, it is imperative that we stand firm in our faith. For there are a myriad of shiny objects that exist for no other purpose than to distract us from our pursuit of Christ.

As men, we can all probably reflect upon a time when we did not stand firm. When we were weak, misguided, or overly enthusiastic and chose the wrong path. We looked the other way, went with the crowd, or acted cowardly by not standing up for what we believed. Which is why it's so important we concentrate on what does matter and ensure we can stand firm when the storms rage. For they will rage!

Journal: The challenge today is for you to ask yourself how you can stand firm in the faith, and what is specifically getting in the way of you standing firm. What does *standing firm* look like for you in your faith, family, work, and life?

_____

_____

_____

_____

_____

_____

_____

_____

_____

_____

_____

_____

_____

_____

_____

_____

_____

_____

Prayer: Let your prayer today be of strength to stand firm in the storm, and the clarity to recognize the storms when they do arise.

DAY 10

BE COURAGEOUS

1 Corinthians 16:14; 14:20; 1 Timothy 2:8

One of our greatest challenges as men is that we have this desire for adventure. We long to be tested, and we push ourselves to see what we are made of. Men need a challenge, and the harder the challenge the more men you will probably have signed up to participate. Ernest Shackleton discovered this trait when he was trying to seek help for his exploration of the South Pole in the early 1900's. He posted a sign reading, "Men wanted for hazardous journey; small wages, bitter cold, long months of complete darkness, constant danger, safe return doubtful, honor and recognition in case of success."

More than 5,000 men answered this call, from sailors to Cambridge-educated scientists, who were probably bored with the life they were living. They longed for a challenge. And while I truly believe that seeking adventure and challenge is a God-given trait, I think it is used all too often in the wrong context or the wrong reasons.

We have this desire in our hearts, but it is tainted by Hollywood's image of a man. We get this perverted image of strength and courage and what a man is supposed to be from the world's standards. We miss the true meaning of what it means to be courageous as a godly man.

Journal: What are the traits of a courageous man? What does courage look like in your life? How do you need to be courageous with your faith, family, and life?

_____

_____

_____

_____

_____

_____

_____

_____

_____

_____

_____

_____

_____

_____

_____

_____

_____

_____

_____

_____

Prayer: Pray today to have the courage to stand in the face of unexpected adventures. Let your foundation for life be in Christ and not the world.

DAY 11

BE STRONG

1 Cor. 16:14; 13:11; Joshua 24:15; 2 Timothy 1:7

We have a very machismo view of "strength" that comes from our own imagination and Hollywood's action movies. We all want to be strong, to save the day, to have what it takes. As men, this is something we all looked for from our fathers, to know that we are strong. If we don't get this validation from our fathers, we become results-driven or a workaholic to prove our worth. Or we become lazy because we know that no matter how hard we worked, it would never be good enough.

And this can also result in us not growing up. Not knowing what it means to be strong can make us hold onto childish things and whims. We men are bad about this, because we love our toys: the trucks, guns, motorcycles, and tools. Now there is nothing wrong with any of these—I enjoy most of them myself. But the real issue becomes the question: "Do we own them, or do they own us?"

A true man is someone who has "put away childish things." A true man knows what is right and stands firm in the fight. A true man is a godly man. He loves the Lord, he loves life, and he loves those whom the Lord has entrusted to his care. A godly man harnesses his strength from God, to overcome the world and their own selfish desires.

Journal: Where do you need to put away childish things, so you can rise up to be a man and have the strength to resist what is of the devil? To achieve this, we need to be able to submit ourselves to God. What part of this submission is difficult for you?

_____

_____

_____

_____

_____

_____

_____

_____

_____

_____

_____

_____

_____

_____

_____

_____

_____

Prayer: Pray today for the strength to be a godly man in a misguided world. Let the clarity of Christ fill your mind with the knowledge and strength of a man following after Christ.

DAY 12

DO EVERYTHING IN LOVE

1 Corinthians 16:14; John 14:15; 1 John 4:7-8

What Paul is basically telling us here is to simply be like Christ, to act like Christ, and to have our actions be reflective of what Christ would do. Yet, as men, we struggle mightily with both love and being Christ-like. We view Christianity as a weakness, when it takes more strength than the average man to maintain.

Until we learn to love well, we will always be showing the world more of us than of Christ. We need to learn to let Christ love others through us instead of fumbling around, attempting to love the unlovable on our own.

As men, we need to do better not only with love—with our wives, children, and each other—but also in being Christ-like. If we cannot act or do everything with love for each other, how are we going to expect to do it with an unbelieving world? And where else are they going to see a vision of what true love looks like?

One of the greatest attributes we can learn as men is to genuinely love as Christ did. To set our selfish desires aside and love others as only Christ can love, and how He has loved us. This trait would be a world-changer by itself.

Journal: My challenge to you today is to dig deep and see what is truly keeping you from love. What does being Christ-like look like to you?

_____
_____
_____
_____
_____
_____
_____
_____
_____
_____
_____
_____
_____
_____
_____
_____
_____
_____
_____

Prayer: Pray today for a deeper understanding of love. Not the kind you see in movies, but true love which can only come from Christ. Pray that you can be a vessel to let Christ love others through you.

DAY 13

BLAMELESS

1 Timothy 3:2

Even though I've heard the word *blameless* a thousand times in my life, I needed a better definition than what I was comprehending. The literal definition is simply "free from blame or guiltless."

This is somewhat of an interesting attribute of a man, because we can carry around a tremendous amount of guilt. From not being home enough, lack of finances, not being there for our wives, or kids. The guilt can mount and become overwhelming at times.

But in this context, we should be free of expecting any guilt placed upon us by others. While we may never live up to our own expectations around how life should be lived, we can still live a life free of blame—if we never put ourselves in situations that could cause blame or guilt to be placed upon us.

I know men who will ride the fine line of danger. Look at a little porn here. Drink too much over there. Let their mind wander to places it should never go. We think this is harmless, but it is not. Seeds are being planted in those moments, which could grow uncontrollably in an instant. Destroying everything they have built by the blame which will be placed upon them because of their thoughtless actions.

Journal: Where do you ride the line of danger in your life? Why do you allow yourself to go to these places? What are some specific steps you can take in order to protect yourself from these places and subsequent guilt?

_____

_____

_____

_____

_____

_____

_____

_____

_____

_____

_____

_____

_____

_____

_____

_____

_____

_____

Prayer: Pray today to be holy as Christ is holy. To truly live a blameless life in all your words, deeds, actions, and responses. Show an unbelieving world what life can truly look like when lived with Christ at the center.

DAY 14

FAITHFUL

1 Timothy 3:2; Luke 16:10

The band *Casting Crowns* has a great song titled, "Broken Together." The song talks about a couple who are trying to make it by the world's standards and failing miserably. The only way they can live whole is to live broken in Christ with each other. This scenario is the only way their relationship could thrive.

Unfortunately, society seems to talk more about men not looking or touching another woman, rather than what it means to truly love their wives. This is a characteristic of men which should be discussed every day. The word *love* used in the Bible is not a suggestion or emotion; it is a command. Which means, it is not something we can opt in and out of as we feel. Love means we are committed to our spouse regardless of the circumstances.

When Paul talks about being faithful, the question becomes: How are you loving, investing, and fully supporting your spouse? Are you creating an environment in your home that is based on the foundation of Christ, and actively growing from that core? The temptation of viewing pornography, committing adultery, and going to places you should not go will slowly disappear the more you put your eyes solely on Christ and love your wife.

Journal: Write out some specific plans or actions you can take in order to love your wife more. How can you implement date nights, surprises, or flowers now and then? What are you going to specifically do to bring the romance back to your relationship?

_____

_____

_____

_____

_____

_____

_____

_____

_____

_____

_____

_____

_____

_____

_____

_____

_____

Prayer: Pray today over your wife and thank God for the gift He gave you in her. Pray specifically over her needs and how you can be more present in her life.

DAY 15

SELF-CONTROL

1 Timothy 3:2; Galatians 5:22-23

Self-control is a challenging subject. As men we would like to think we have control over our actions. But in reality, we're all probably a little challenged in this area. Whether it's a weak moment alone in a hotel room with the TV or computer. Or not being strong enough to stand up at the right time for our wives or children. Having too many drinks, not watching our mouth, or where our eyes may wander. There are 100 different ways we don't have self-control, and these open a little door to darkness in our hearts.

The problem is we attempt to control our lives on our own—which is a dangerous path to travel. Our self-control will come from selflessly putting our focus on Christ and Christ alone. Our feeble attempts to try this based upon our own power will always end in disastrous results.

Stop attempting to take on every battle yourself and find true self-control. Spend time in the Bible, pray, and fix your eyes on Jesus. Building a lifestyle of living in Christ will let the old things pass away so you can focus on what is new, right, good, and life-giving. This will give you the control you need far beyond your own capabilities.

Journal: Write down those areas of your life where you struggle with self-control (i.e. lust, drinking, language, wandering eyes, etc.). Once you have your list, can you identify why these are issues for you?

_____

_____

_____

_____

_____

_____

_____

_____

_____

_____

_____

_____

_____

_____

_____

_____

_____

Prayer: Pray today for a complete cleansing from God and ask that He fills you up. May the old life be pushed out because there is no room left in your life for those old habits.

DAY 16

LIVE WISELY

1 Timothy 3:2; 1 Corinthians 13:11

I don't know about you, but I feel I do something stupid about once a day. You would think that at this point in my life, there would be some wisdom that comes along with my age. But that is not always the case. Living wisely is a daily concentration which takes effort regardless of our circumstances.

Too often, we are tempted by the shiny objects of life, which challenge us in our wise thinking. The nice car, bigger house, more expensive clothes, shoes, bikes, toys, or equipment can always tempt us to live foolishly. We purchase things we don't need, with money we don't have, to impress people we don't even like. Unlike other areas of our lives, we don't seem to learn from these experiences. We repeat them over and over, often with greater severity than the last.

Living wisely means making decisions based upon the community's needs and not Self. Which is a daily struggle of overcoming Self. What is best for the family, church, or community is your focus, which in some cases may come in direct contradiction to your desires. By daily taking up your cross to have the mindset of Christ instead of your own, you are choosing to live wisely and in Christ, instead of foolishly for yourself.

Journal: Write down the times when you've lived foolishly in your life. What are the objects that make you spend money unnecessarily? Can you identify why these items make you live foolishly?

_____

_____

_____

_____

_____

_____

_____

_____

_____

_____

_____

_____

_____

_____

_____

_____

_____

_____

_____

_____

Prayer: Pray today for a strong heart and mind to live wisely in Christ. Put the foolish things aside to concentrate on the life Christ has for you and not your own agenda.

DAY 17

GOOD REPUTATION

1 Timothy 3:2; Proverbs 22:1

Recently, we have witnessed how many accomplished men's empires and reputations have been destroyed because of their actions. From Harvey Weinstein, Bill Cosby, Kevin Spacey, and the list goes on and on. Men who thought they were untouchable and could get away with anything have had everything taken away from them, including their reputation, because of their actions.

Your reputation is built upon your actions. And many men are one step away from a complete implosion.

What do other people say about you when you're not around? Although this may not be a question you dwell on regularly, you have probably considered its ramifications from time to time. Our actions, words, and responses all have a lasting effect on others in either a positive or negative way.

The irony of a reputation is that if you are following after God's own heart, then you are building a solid reputation in the process. When you love others by seeking first His kingdom, the result is you become more patient, kind, and gentle. In the end, you will gain the reputation of someone who cares and can be trusted—because your reputation is built upon Christ and not on anything in this world.

Journal: Write out what you think others would say about your reputation. Do you like what you see? Ask a friend or two to write this out for you to see what they would say. What areas of your life and reputation do you need to work on and begin building up? How will you start this process?

_____

_____

_____

_____

_____

_____

_____

_____

_____

_____

_____

_____

_____

_____

_____

_____

Prayer: Pray today that you could truly live a life in Christ. Don't pray for a better reputation but pray that your life would be so in line with what Christ wants for you that your reputation will be built upon that center.

DAY 18

HOSPITABLE

1 Timothy 3:2; Hebrews 10:25

I have a few good friends who always have the outdoor fireplace lit, a glass of scotch, and fine cigar waiting whenever I visit. This is highlighted by a late night of great conversation. These are moments I cherish dearly. While hospitality is a trait generally associated with women, its goal and purpose are just as necessary and vital for men.

Men don't congregate and talk like women do. But that doesn't mean we shouldn't be getting together more. I'm eternally grateful for the friends who create these environments where we can talk, laugh, and discuss the deeper questions of life. For that is what life is all about. Those deep moments of conversation, which usually come out of someone being hospitable.

You can probably reflect on some of your more enjoyable moments. Those times of belly laughs, late nights, and deep, much-needed conversations. Moments like those are usually sparked by some invitation. Someone invited you, or you invited others, into that moment. A moment that can forge a lasting memory and experience in your life.

What is stopping you from creating much-needed moments like those more often?

Journal: Write out those moments in life that were memorable to you. Who invited you into those times? What does being hospitable mean to you? Is this a trait you need to be more intentional about?

_____

_____

_____

_____

_____

_____

_____

_____

_____

_____

_____

_____

_____

_____

_____

_____

_____

_____

Prayer: Pray today for opportunities to be more hospitable to a core group of men around you. Pray that God would open some doors for you to reach, minister, and connect to a group wherein everyone can truly grow together.

DAY 19

BE ABLE TO TEACH

1 Timothy 3:2; Matthew 28:20

I have vivid memories of being around 5 or 6 years old and going to my grandfather's house where my grandpa would always let me shoot his BB gun. For hours we would be out back while he taught me how to shoot. He never seemed to mind walking down the makeshift range to set back up the cans we had knocked over. His patience and instruction were valuable to me and I got increasingly better with the BB gun every time I visited.

You were probably taught something by your father, a coach, or other men in your life. Even though many of these men would not have considered themselves teachers, being able to teach others is a valuable part of being a man. I learned how to fish, drive a car, and how to be a man from my father. In the process of these learning experiences, there was not a lot of actual "classroom-type" teaching, we were just doing life together. But this is an aspect of being a Thrival Man we need to hang onto dearly.

You have some gift, talent, or ability you can teach and pass on to a whole new generation. Don't undermine your gift or your ability to teach your gift to others. Investing in someone else's life, someone who knows you care and are giving them something useful, is invaluable.

Journal: Begin the process of writing out your gifts, talents, and abilities. Then take the time to do some research to find out where you can teach these skills to others. Either with your kids, in church, a camp, after-school programs, or setting up your own time. No matter where, be intentional about teaching from your heart to impress the next generation.

_____

_____

_____

_____

_____

_____

_____

_____

_____

_____

_____

_____

_____

_____

_____

_____

Prayer: Pray today over your skills and abilities and that God would open a door for you to discover places where you can teach others.

DAY 20

NOT A HEAVY DRINKER

1 Timothy 3:3

During my stints of working in the corporate world, there were inevitable times of parties, gatherings, and conferences. I was generally amazed at how much alcohol some of my colleagues could consume (especially my British co-workers). Then they would show up the next morning at work bright and cheery. I'm not sure how they accomplished such feats, but I assumed it was through years of practice.

If you read the Bible long enough, you know that it is a book of moderation. Drinking is the same. This is not a condemnation on whether you drink or not—that is between you and God. But how much you drink can have ramifications affecting other aspects of you being a man. I never met a man who confided in me all the great, moral, and upright things he accomplished the more he drank. The outcome is usually quite the contrary.

In the attempt to be a man of character and build up a good reputation, this is certainly an aspect of your life you need to consider, which is not discussed enough. How much do you drink? How often do you drink? Even, why do you drink? These are legitimate questions only you can answer. These can have a lasting impact on your reputation in becoming a truly thriving man.

Journal: Simply ask yourself the question of why you drink. Then begin to reflect on who your drinking affects directly in your life. Follow this thought out to see where it leads you in the understanding of your own habits. If you don't drink, think of other vices in your life adversely affecting you.

_____

_____

_____

_____

_____

_____

_____

_____

_____

_____

_____

_____

_____

_____

_____

_____

Prayer: Let your prayer today be one of leaving your vice at the foot of the cross. Again, this is really between you and God. What does He have to say to you? How has it affected your life in the past, and what type of man does God need you to be moving forward?

DAY 21

VIOLENCE AND ANGER

1 Timothy 3:3; Proverbs 4:23

During an extremely painful time in my own life, the filter in my head, which keeps me rational was completely gone. The intense physical pain I was suffering had stripped any ability to control anger, outbursts, or situations beyond my control. It came to the point where we had to sit our children down and explain to them I was not myself, and to ask forgiveness beforehand for my actions.

One night I unloaded on my oldest son, who was 10 at the time, for something extremely insignificant in the grand scheme of life. My heart was crushed as he sat there in front of me, bawling as he said, "I know this is not you." Seeing firsthand the result of your anger is an extremely humiliating and humbling place to be.

Controlling our anger is another aspect that plays into the good reputation part of being a man. If you are prone to violent outbursts, your children become afraid of you, or others speak poorly of you behind your back. Then this is certainly a condition of your life that needs to be more broadly explored. Our actions have a lasting impression on our children and those around us. If they are not positive, then we must explore the basis and reasoning behind the outbursts.

Journal: Write out those times when you have had violent outbursts. Can you write out why you lost it? What happened to cause you to react in such a manner? We usually act in this way due to someone questioning our manhood in one way or another. Was this your problem?

_____

_____

_____

_____

_____

_____

_____

_____

_____

_____

_____

_____

_____

_____

_____

_____

_____

_____

Prayer: Pray today for the peace which passes all understanding to fill every part of your life. To be filled with Christ so much there is no room for the hate and anger of the world to penetrate that part of your life.

DAY 22

GENTLE

1 Timothy 3:3; Galatians 5:22-23

Generally, being gentle is not viewed as a very manly trait. Men are supposed to be rough, tough, and ready to pounce on anything that comes their way. The truth is, those aspects of being a man should always be balanced with a gentle spirit. For if we don't possess the right balance, then we are merely ramming our way through circumstances in order to always tip the scales in our favor.

Learning to possess a gentle spirit is truly a God-given gift. I'm in awe of the few men I know who display this trait in an open and manly way. The irony is that other men are generally drawn to these individuals because they know they are safe. Every man needs a place to lay down their burdens, and the men who have the gentle spirit are usually the ones who can handle these burdens appropriately.

But we all must display these traits when it comes to our wives, children, and friends. While this can be challenging at times, we must learn to harness gentleness as a God-given gift to share with others. Being gentle is one of the greatest traits we can possess in order to invite others into the true meaning of living like Christ. For a gentle man is one who carries the concerns of others with great care. Why else would we be referred to as *gentlemen*?

Journal: Write out today how you are gentle. Are there places in your life where you could improve? What would a gentle spirit really look like in your life?

_____

_____

_____

_____

_____

_____

_____

_____

_____

_____

_____

_____

_____

_____

_____

_____

_____

_____

_____

Prayer: Pray today for a gentle spirit. The forces of this world are constantly working against anything gentle. Pray for a breakthrough in order to possess and show a gentle spirit to family, friends, and the community.

DAY 23

NOT QUARRELSOME

1 Timothy 3:3; James 1:19

I worked several years with this one guy who would argue with anyone about anything. The topic of discussion did not matter as he had some differing point of view he had to throw into the conversation. Apparently, he was incapable of agreeing with you on any opinion you might possess. His attitude was exhausting. Constantly attempting to have a conversation and navigating his quarrelsome spirit was a drain on everyone around him.

You probably know someone like this in your own life. When you argue and engage in this type of behavior, you're generally attempting to defend yourself. You argue because you have to be right, and you have a desire to defend your little kingdom no matter the cost.

But when you look at Christ, even though He was falsely accused, beaten, with rumors spread about him, and ultimately hung on a cross, He never once attempted to defend himself or argue the attacks of his accusers. Mainly because it would not have mattered. Do you really think the Pharisees would have changed their minds due to a whimsical retort from Jesus? But think about the situation: if Christ never attempted to argue His own defense, then why are you?

Journal: Why do you argue? What are some specific instances where you exerted a lot of energy to defend something related to yourself? Why did you argue? What were you attempting to prove? What were you defending? What were some other ways you could have used to handle the situation differently?

_____

_____

_____

_____

_____

_____

_____

_____

_____

_____

_____

_____

_____

_____

_____

_____

Prayer: Pray today that your life could be so ingrained in Christ that you have no need to defend yourself. That your identity would be found in Christ and not in the world. Pray that daily you could always be taking a step closer to the cross.

DAY 24

NOT LOVE MONEY

1 Timothy 3:3; Matthew 6:21

Most men will not come right out and admit they love money, although there are a few. But as men, we really do love our stuff. The tools, off-road vehicles, gadgets, gizmos, and electronics. Nothing is fast enough, loud enough, or good enough for us. We will spend an exorbitant amount of money to purchase these toys.

Now there's nothing wrong with these toys, they're just objects. The reasoning behind why we purchase such items is really the topic we must explore. Do we need to prove something to someone else? Do we need to prove value to ourselves? Do we feel less of a man if we don't have these things? For if we are pursuing these items to fulfill some need that should only be filled by Christ, then we are being distracted by the shiny objects of money and stuff.

This is an interesting characteristic Paul chooses to highlight in this passage. If your focus is on your toys, then you have to make a lot of money. Thus, this becomes your primary focus. Spending a life focused on Christ becomes secondary to your ability to make and spend money. For where you find your treasure is truly where you heart will be. Either in pursuing money or being like Christ. Which do you choose?

Journal: Write out today all your toys or where your money goes. Go to your bank account if necessary to see where you spend your money. When you look at your items, how necessary are they in your life? Could you do without them? Write out alternate uses for your money. For having a lot of money is not a sin, but how it rules your heart can be.

_____

_____

_____

_____

_____

_____

_____

_____

_____

_____

_____

_____

_____

_____

Prayer: Let your prayer today be one of freeing you up from your money. That you could find contentment in your life with what you have, and you can spend your time and resources on the Kingdom of God instead of your own little kingdom.

DAY 25

MANAGE YOUR HOUSEHOLD

1 Timothy 3:4-5

There are days where I feel like I'm only maintaining our household but not managing it very well. For instance, when I'm writhing in pain with deadlines looming. Or my wife is working late and the kids all seem to have separate activities all over town. Life can get chaotic quickly. Which is exactly the reason why it's important to manage my household well.

I have known many men who were extremely successful in their work. They could close large deals, influence boardrooms, and rally the staff during challenging projects. Yet, their homes were a disaster. Their wives were bitter, their children didn't talk to them, and their home was in genuine disarray. Why is it a man who is so successful at work can fail so miserably at home? The result is usually directly correlated to the time they invest in their home and family.

This is why it's extremely important to manage your household. To be intentional with your family, invest your time at home instead of other pursuits. The legacy you leave with your family will last far longer than anything you accomplish at work. For how can you ever share the love of Christ with others and show them a life well-lived, if your own home does not reflect those characteristics?

Journal: Spend time today thinking about your home. Does it need some straightening up? What needs to happen first? What can you control and what do you need help with?

_____

_____

_____

_____

_____

_____

_____

_____

_____

_____

_____

_____

_____

_____

_____

_____

_____

_____

Prayer: Say a prayer of protection over your house today. That the Spirit of God would cover your house in a hedge of protection (Job 1:10) and break through any strongholds on your home. Then pray for the wisdom and strength to lead your home wisely.

DAY 26

CUTTING OUT THE NOISE

Ephesians 6:19; Hebrews 12:1-2

Acting for Self is easy. Selfish actions and responses really take no effort or forethought on our part. We simply just act to serve ourselves however we can. But if we want to be a real man, it's going to take time, effort, and patience on your part. Which is probably why we see so few real Thrival Men. It is a difficult pursuit.

With so much noise out there telling us who we should be as men, it can become increasingly difficult to sift through the clutter to find a valid response. From action movies, social media, consumer items, or old tales, we can find a varied response to what our lives should look like as men. But if we pursue these definitions, we will always be wanting more when it comes to our own lives.

This is why it's important to always return to the foundation of the Bible when it comes to your definition of a man. To look at the life of Christ and see how he spoke, treated others, and lived. This is the purest definition of what it really means to be a man of God. There is no clutter or noise involved. Just the purity of what it means to live a life in Christ. But remember, the image Christ set as a man is in direct contradiction to the definition you see in society. Which is why you must cut out the noise.

Journal: Write out your Biblical definition of a man. What are the traits? How do they act, speak, or live? How are they as a husband, father, or worker? Draw a clear picture of what it really means to be a godly man in today's modern world.

_____

_____

_____

_____

_____

_____

_____

_____

_____

_____

_____

_____

_____

_____

_____

_____

_____

_____

Prayer: Pray that you would be able to live like Christ in today's world. To drop the clutter and messages of this world in order to live the life built with the center for Christ.

DAY 27

LIVING WITH PURPOSE

Ephesians 6:19; John 5:19-23

Throughout history, man's attempt to domesticate warriors has rarely gone well. Whether it be the American Indians or African tribes. When we took away the purpose of the men in the tribe, the results were generally the same. When the men lacked purpose, it took away hope. The men eventually resided themselves to drinking and lying around all day doing nothing.

Purpose is a powerful tool for a man. Most men need this driving force in order to find success. The problem is, men seldom find their purpose in God. They will exert a tremendous amount of energy for work, finances, or play. But not in discovering how to live out their purpose in Christ. When we find our purpose outside of Christ, we are constantly chasing fruitless pursuits.

Our purpose in life should be built upon the foundation which is Christ. Then upon that foundation our purpose in work, marriage, parenting, and life are built upon the solid footing of Christ. There is no other way to make sense of this crazy world than by living out your purpose in Christ.

What drives you to pursue the success you achieve in life? Can you find your purpose in Christ?

Journal: What is your purpose? Can you define it? What are your traits, what drives you? Write out the gifts, talents, and abilities God has given you, and discover your purpose in Christ.

_____

_____

_____

_____

_____

_____

_____

_____

_____

_____

_____

_____

_____

_____

_____

_____

_____

_____

Prayer: Pray today over your purpose. But don't put too much pressure on yourself. God is bigger than any plan or idea you might create. Simply pray for peace and understanding about your life in Christ and that you do not miss opportunities to see where He is working all around you.

DAY 28

FINDING YOUR TREASURE

Ephesians 6:20; Luke 12:33-34

For many years now, men have been going to work to find their treasure. Only to realize it wasn't there, so they begin seeking other places to find their treasure. This catch in our spirit has caused many men to pursue unhealthy and treacherous adventures since Adam and Eve in the Garden of Eden.

Men have a longing for challenge and adventure, to find the treasure that always seems to be churning at the depths of their soul. The problem is, when we turn to the world to fill this void, we won't be satisfied. We will constantly go to the ends of the world to find our treasure. But it is a treasure that can only be filled with Christ.

We make time for what is important to us. When men tell me they just don't have time to spend with God, I see they have time to golf, ride bikes, hike, take trips, and play. So surely, they do have time for God. Their treasure is in the wrong place, and their pursuits in life reveal their heart. There is no more important treasure than putting your life fully and completely in Christ.

When looking at the life in Christ, stop thinking of what you have to give up; instead, define it by the amazing treasure you receive in Christ. (Matt. 13:44)

Journal: Where is your treasure? Where do you put your time, money, and resources? Do you feel you have set aside time for God every day? What is your greatest obstacle to pursuing Christ with all your heart, soul, mind, and strength?

_____

_____

_____

_____

_____

_____

_____

_____

_____

_____

_____

_____

_____

_____

_____

_____

_____

Prayer: Pray today to have a heart that is centered on the one and only treasure. Pray that the distractions on this life can be removed in order for you to see the treasure clearly.

DAY 29

UNDISTRACTED LIVING

Ephesians 6:20; Romans 8:28

You probably experience distractions regularly to the point where you don't even notice them anymore. You get up and read the news. Go to your job for 8 to 10 hours fully embedded in the work of your company. You come home and surf the Internet, check social media, work on your car, take the kids to activities, or watch your favorite team. Every second of your day is filled with some activity that's keeping you from a greater work you could accomplish.

This is the greatest tool of the Devil. He doesn't have to make you into a monster, he just has to keep you so busy and distracted you don't have time for Christ in your life. And he has done an excellent job. Think about the greater work you could be doing in teaching, serving, raising young men up, or being a witness to others. Yet, you are too "busy" to spend time on what matters most to the Kingdom of God.

The distractions in your life are all around you, are not going to magically disappear, and will more than likely grow larger every year. Stop thinking about what you might have to give up in the process and focus more on the treasure. What will you gain in your time, experience, and life by living it fully in Christ, instead of the thousand different ways the world suggests you live?

Journal: Start listing out the distractions in your life. (e.g. social media, Internet, hobbies, news, etc.) How often do you spend time on these distractions? How often do you engage in these distractions when you should be doing something else? List 3 distractions and then eliminate them today.

_____

_____

_____

_____

_____

_____

_____

_____

_____

_____

_____

_____

_____

_____

_____

_____

Prayer: Pray today for the focus to concentrate on Christ and the strength to eliminate any distraction keeping you from your focus.

DAY 30

THE THRIVAL MAN

Ephesians 6:10-18; 1 Corinthians 16:13-14

There are many suggestions, ideas, and thoughts out there about what it means to be a man. Most of them are self-seeking and will eventually lead to some sort of destruction. As men, we were created in the image of our Creator to be more than we could ever imagine. We were called as His workmanship to do more than Christ did on this earth. That is mind blowing. Yet, most men are simply surviving life just hoping something will change—maybe a promotion, win the lottery, or life will calm down. Some magical event that'll make everything better.

Christ is calling you to the greatest adventure you can imagine. A story far beyond anything you could ever create yourself. Jesus did not come to earth as a man, be betrayed, beaten, and hung on a cross so you could simply survive life. He has called you to *thrive*. To live an abundant life in him. This is your life.

The life of a Thrival Man is to reject the message of the world and live a life in Christ in service to others. To not just survive life and hope for the best. Throw off your chains, stand up in force, and join a growing tribe of men who choose Christ first and to live all out for Him. This is the call of the Thrival Man!

Journal: How are you just surviving life right now? How can you begin to live as a Thrival Man today? What are your greatest obstacles? How can you overcome these obstacles? What is the first step you can take today?

_____

_____

_____

_____

_____

_____

_____

_____

_____

_____

_____

_____

_____

_____

_____

_____

_____

_____

_____

Prayer: Pray that you can live a life fully in Christ. Pray for other brothers to be raised up around you, and to build your own tribe and live an abundant life as a Thrival Man.

ENDNOTES

Henry David Thoreau, "Henry David Thoreau," Wik-iQuotes.com, http://bit.ly/2PTMg9p, accessed on August 29, 2018.

Day 3: Your Responsibility as a Man
- *Osborne, C., & McLanahan, S. (2007). Partnership instability and child well-being. Journal of Marriage and Family, 69, 1065-1083* http://bit.ly/2MsUtPs.

Day 8: Work Enthusiastically
- Cayla Vidmar, "The Construction Flagger People Can't Help but Love," The Crested Butte News, http://bit.ly/2wunW5F, accessed on August 29, 2018.

Day 10: Be Courageous
- Paul Coughlin, "No More Christian Nice Guy," (Bloomington, Illinois, Bethany House Publishers, 2016), p.20.

Day 13: Blameless
- "blameless," Dictionary.com, https://www.dictionary.com/browse/blameless?s=t, accessed on August 21, 2018.

Day 17: Good Reputation

- Pamela Engel, "Bill Cosby's sexual-assault trial starts today – here's the backstory of the allegations against him," BusinessInsider.com, http://read.bi/2i5kqdK, accessed on October 11, 2017.
- Sasha Savitsky, "Harvey Weinstein accused of raping 3 women, sexually harassing Gwyneth Paltrow, Angelina Jolie," Fox News, FoxNews.com, http://fxn.ws/2yb37OO, accessed on October 11, 2017.
- Maria Puente, "Kevin Spacy Scandal: A complete list of the 15 accusers," USAToday, USAToday.com, https://usat.ly/2C1rtOb, accessed on August 30,2018.

Join the Thrival Man Tribe

Do you want to work directly with Eric? Let Eric guide you through the process of eliminating distractions to live a better story!

This task is accomplished through retreats, devotionals, videos, and more content.

You can be part of an individual or group coaching, enlist in one of *The Thrival Man* retreats, or connect with our online community. Participants can join from anywhere in the world.

**Join our newsletter to keep
up to date at
THETHRIVALMAN.COM**

BRING ERIC INTO
your business or organization

SPEAKER | AUTHOR

Eric understands the challenge of finding the right speaker for an event, bringing the correct topic, and the importance of engaging the audience. As a consultant, business leader, and former pastor, Eric knows the success of any event can easily hinge on the quality of the speaker.

Eric is keenly aware of the need to engage with the audience, equip them with practical takeaways, and provide a different perspective on creating a better adventure. He customizes each message and training to achieve and exceed the objectives of his clients.

Contact Eric today at:
EricPEaton.com

Learn more about

KNIGHTS OF HEROES:

www.knightsofheroes.org

ABOUT THE AUTHOR

Eric teaches men how to eliminate distractions, helping them to create a better adventure in their own lives to live a thriving life. Through his writing, speaking, and coaching, Eric empowers men to realize they are not alone in their struggles.

Understanding the need to raise up more godly men in this world, Eric is dedicated in his commitment to guide men to a thriving life.

Eric started out early in his career, blazing a quick trail of success as a consultant. However, he was sidelined by a hip reconstruction surgery, which left him in chronic pain since the age of 27. Eric has spent the last few years helping people deal with their own obstacles and struggles, which made him realize how many men are weighed down with their own distractions without a path to move forward.

Eric wants to show those who live with limitations that their lives have meaning and purpose. Through his speaking and writing, he is committed to direct people toward their own path to a better adventure. Eric and his wife Erica live in the mountains of Colorado and are blessed with three awesome teenagers.

Connect at: **EricPEaton.com**

CPSIA information can be obtained
at www.ICGtesting.com
Printed in the USA
LVHW041024121118
596787LV00021BC/516/P